Have a great day.

Made in the USA
Monee, IL
07 December 2019

18118380R00069